LARRY BURKETT

SOUND INVESTMENTS

MOODY PRESS
CHICAGO

© 1991 by
CHRISTIAN FINANCIAL CONCEPTS

Compiled from material originally published by Christian Financial Concepts, Inc.

All Scripture quotations, unless noted otherwise, are from the *New American Standard Bible*, © 1960, 1962, 1963, 1968, 1971, 1972, 1973, 1975, and 1977 by The Lockman Foundation, and are used by permission.

ISBN: 0-8024-2600-X

3 4 5 6 Printing/VP/Year 95 94 93 92

Printed in the United States of America

About the Author

Larry Burkett is committed to teaching God's people His principles for managing money. Unfortunately, money management is one area often neglected by Christians, and it is a major cause of conflict and disruption in both business and family life.

For more than two decades Larry has counseled and taught God's principles for finance across the country. As director of Christian Financial Concepts, Larry has counseled, conducted seminars, and written numerous books on the subject of maintaining control of the budget. In additon he is heard on more than 1000 radio outlets worldwide.

Sound Investments

PURPOSES OF INVESTING

I was asked a penetrating question by a close Christian friend: "Why should we help rich people get richer?" The obvious answer is that teaching Christians to invest wisely is as necessary as teaching them to budget. God has commissioned us to help Christians become better stewards, which includes using our surplus resources properly. It is obvious that those with a surplus are able to give more to God's work than are others. One function of any ministry of finances is teaching Christians how and why to multiply their resources for giving.

HISTORY OF INVESTING

The first investment can be found in Genesis 3:23. Adam was cast out of the Garden and told to cultivate the soil for food. To do so he had to risk planting seeds that could have been eaten; thus he became an investor. Farmers understand the principle of investing. Each year they are faced with a choice of eating all their seeds, selling all their seeds, or retaining some to replant. It is a short-sighted farmer who either eats or sells his entire harvest. He would still have some harvest the next season from the seed that fell during picking, but it would be pretty slim. A wise farmer not only holds some seed for replanting, but he also sorts out the best seed to insure a greater harvest. By doing so he exercises self-discipline to achieve greater prosperity.

Contrary to what many people believe, God is not against prosperity. The Scriptures give evidence that one of God's blessings to those who love and obey Him is prosperity (2 Chronicles 16:9; Psalm 37:4).

To allow material assets to erode through bad management is not good stewardship. It's a sign of slothfulness. But if you multiply and store them without purpose, you are guilty of hoarding like the rich fool in Luke 12.

JUSTIFICATION FOR INVESTING

A rational reason for not investing a surplus is to give it away to further God's work and to help the needy. However, there is no evidence in the Bible that God's plan is for us always to give away surplus. In fact, the opposite is true. Saving is a sign of wisdom, whereas lack is a sign of slothfulness. "There is precious treasure and oil in the dwelling of the wise, but a foolish man swallows it up" (Proverbs 21:20). There are exceptions, but they are individual directives, not biblical principles.

In Matthew 25:14-30 several references are made to investing various amounts. In our economy the largest amount mentioned, five talents, would be equal to approximately $1,784,000, and the smallest, one talent, would be about $356,835. The intent of this parable is to reflect on the attitudes and faithfulness of investors in the absence of their master. Each was rewarded or punished according to his stewardship. If investing is prohibited or even discouraged, why did Jesus use it as an example and reward the most diligent? The answer is that investing is another part of stewardship—not more important than giving but not less important either.

PREREQUISITES FOR INVESTING

The number one prerequisite for investing is the proper attitude. Why are you investing, and how will the surplus be used? If a Christian wants to be entrusted with greater riches, he must be found faithful in the smaller amounts first (Luke 16:10-11).

The term used throughout Paul's writings is *contentment*. "But godliness actually is a means of great gain, when accompanied by contentment" (1 Timothy 6:6). In a society oriented toward "more" and "best" it is difficult to reach the right balance.

The most important thing to remember is that it's wrong to invest just for the sake of making money. Making money should be a by-product of doing what God has called you to do. Also remember that peace does not come through the accumulation of material possessions; if it did, the wealthiest people in the world would be the most at peace. Instead, they're often frustrated and miserable. True peace comes only from God. "Peace I leave with you; My peace I give to you; not as the world gives, do I give to you. Let not your heart be troubled, nor let it be fearful" (John 14:27).

Another important principle to remember when considering any type of investing is that we are to be stewards, literally managers, of another's property. More specifically, we are the managers of God's property. It's good to recall what Paul said to Timothy: "For we have brought nothing into the world, so we cannot take anything out of it either" (1 Timothy 6:7). It's not how much you accumulate that's important, it's how it is being used.

COMMITMENT TO A PLAN

To protect against the infectious diseases of greed and pride, the best weapon is a specific plan for returning your excess income to God's kingdom. I find that once a commitment has been made to a disciplined lifestyle, regardless of available income, the danger of greed and self-indulgence is drastically reduced.

Even within the church the examples of those acting as good stewards of surplus resources are few. It is critical to develop a godly plan to allocate profits based upon wise investment of the surplus instead of only learning to invest what you have now.

One interesting characteristic about humans is that we can rationalize nearly anything, including reinvesting God's portion or "saving" it for Him. Therefore it is important to settle on a plan for distributing the profits from investments before they arrive. Decide what portion is to be reinvested. Clearly the greatest danger is to continually reinvest the profits and rationalize it because of taxes, lack of discernible needs, or a need for surplus security. Do your planning before the money becomes available. One good way to do that is to give away a large percentage of the investment before it appreciates. "Because of the proof given by this ministry they will glorify God for your obedience to your confession of the gospel of Christ, and for the liberality of your contribution to them and to all" (2 Corinthians 9:13).

LEGITIMATE REASONS FOR INVESTING

There are several legitimate reasons for a Christian to invest.

1. TO FURTHER GOD'S WORK

Some Christians have received a gift of giving (Romans 12:8). To them, the multiplication of material worth

Larry Burkett

is an extension of their ministry within the Body of Christ. Even for those who do not have a gift of giving, investments are a way to preserve and multiply a surplus that has been provided. In Acts 4:32-37 the believers sell their assets and surrender the proceeds to meet the needs of other believers. God blesses some with surplus to be used at a later date. (For more on giving, see *Giving and Tithing* in this series.)

As you learn to invest money according to God's principles, you'll find that God will increase your opportunity to help other people. That is, in reality, the true purpose of investing—to increase your assets so that you can serve God more fully. If you do as the rich fool did and tear down your barns to build larger ones, expect God to deal with you as He did with him. "God said to him, 'You fool! This very night your soul is required of you; and now who will own what you have prepared?'" (Luke 12:20). We are all accountable to God for everything we do, including how we manage His money.

2. FAMILY RESPONSIBILITY

We are admonished to provide for those within our own households

11

(1 Timothy 5:8). That provision was not limited to a man's lifetime. It extended to providing for his family even after his death. Not everyone can do so, but if the able provide for the needs of their families, the church can concentrate on the needs of the poor. "If a man fathers a hundred children and lives many years, however many they be, but his soul is not satisfied with good things, and he does not even have a proper burial, then I say, 'Better the miscarriage than he'" (Ecclesiastes 6:3).

If parents believe that God wants their children to go to college, is it more spiritual to expect the government and banks to pay for their education than to store for the eventual need? The parable of the ant in Proverbs 6:6 says to "observe her ways and be wise." One of her ways is to plan ahead by storing. In a highly inflationary economy even storing requires investing.

So a legitimate purpose for any investment program is to help your family achieve a greater degree of security. This can include investing to provide for your children's education, an inheritance for your family, or retirement. (See *Personal Finances* for further discussion of budgets and financial planning.)

But there are also nonscriptural reasons for investing—greed, envy, pride, and ignorance, to name a few.

ILLEGITIMATE REASONS FOR INVESTING

Unfortunately these unbiblical reasons motivate the greater number of investors, Christian and non-Christian alike, because Satan so dominates our attitudes about money.

GREED

Greed is the consistent desire to have more and demand the best. "But those who want to get rich fall into temptation and a snare and many foolish and harmful desires which plunge men into ruin and destruction" (1 Timothy 6:9).

ENVY

Envy is the desire to achieve, based on observing other people's success. "For I was envious of the arrogant, as I saw the prosperity of the wicked" (Psalm 73:3).

PRIDE

Pride is the desire to be elevated

because of material achievements. "Instruct those who are rich in this present world not to be conceited or to fix their hope on the uncertainty of riches, but on God, who richly supplies us with all things to enjoy" (1 Timothy 6:17).

IGNORANCE

Ignorance is following the counsel of other misguided people because you lack discernment. "Leave the presence of a fool, or you will not discern words of knowledge" (Proverbs 14:7).

There are many wrong motives for investing. Acting on any of these causes anxiety, frustration, and eventually a deadening of spiritual values. As our Lord says, "No servant can serve two masters; for either he will hate the one, and love the other, or else he will hold to one and despise the other. You cannot serve God and mammon" (Luke 16:13).

DECIDING HOW MUCH TO INVEST

Once a Christian has accepted the biblical purposes of investing, the crucial decision is how much to invest. Obviously there is no universal answer. It is an individual decision that each Christian makes after much prayer. With earnest prayer a wise decision is difficult—without it, impossible. Some initial choices must be made that will greatly simplify the decision about how much to invest.

1. Before investing, give to God's work until you know that all of the needs God has placed on your heart are satisfied. Don't be misled into thinking that there will then be no more needs in the world. There will always be needs, but God doesn't place every need on every person's heart. Giving, like spiritual discernment, is a matter of growth and practice. I believe the key is: When in doubt, give. It is better to be wrong and give too much than to ignore God's direction and give too little. The Spirit is never dampened by too sensitive a will. "Openly before the churches show them the proof of your love and of our reason for boasting about you" (2 Corinthians 8:24).

2. Settle on a level of family needs that is God's plan for you. Too much spending on a family can rob surplus funds as surely as bad investments. Each Christian family must decide on the level that God has planned for them and stick to it in spite of available surplus. Remember the need for bal-

ance. Too much is waste; too little is self-punishment. "Whatever we ask we receive from Him, because we keep His commandments and do the things that are pleasing in His sight" (1 John 3:22).

WHY BOTHER WITH COUNSEL?

The purpose of counsel is to aid us in making our decisions, not to actually make them for us. Too often we want someone to tell us what to do. When you allow someone else to tell you what to do, with rare exception you're going to get bad advice. Many people have told me that an adviser told them to buy a particular investment that ended up losing money, but the adviser made money through the purchase. Sometimes the advice is both right and wrong, as in the recent instance of a Christian couple who bought into a whiskey-aging partnership—the investment was great (about 25 to 30 percent growth per year), but not for Christians. Under a strong conviction about being both stewards and witnesses, they ended up selling out at a sizable loss. The other investors will probably end up making a sizable profit over the next ten years. The investment advice was accurate; the counsel was entirely wrong.

SELECTING GOOD COUNSEL

A commonly asked question is, "How can I find good Christian counsel?" But perhaps even more fundamental would be the question, "How can I tell when I find good Christian counsel?"

No single financial plan will fit every family. Unfortunately, today there are many financial planners who tend to press everybody into one mold. I believe in using financial advisers, and I encourage you to use professionals in areas of law, accounting, and financial planning. The key is to use them as sources of expertise, not gurus. They can provide alternatives, suggestions, and expert advice, but ultimately you must make your own decisions.

There are basically two types of financial advisers. One gives advice and charges a fee for it. The other sells financial products in the process of giving advice. I consider the latter more a salesman than a counselor. Salesmen have a place in the planning process, particularly in selecting investments, but they should not be used as primary counsel. Although there is nothing wrong with product sales, eventually a counselor will sell you the product he represents. He believes in his product and rightly so, but diversity as prescribed in Ecclesiastes 11:2 requires a broader array of investments than one salesman can offer.

For instance, it would be difficult to obtain objective counsel about which car would best suit your family's needs from a salesman who earns his living selling Hondas. He is going to be biased by his sales training, experience, and especially by his need to sell a Honda. A good salesman will match his product to your need as closely as possible and will seldom suggest you look elsewhere.

The bias toward a particular product is only one limitation in finding good counsel. Another critical issue is finding counselors with "like" minds and attitudes, namely Christians. What makes it even more difficult is that many counselors who profess to be Christians give unwise advice.

I can understand the difficulty and frustration of locating good Christian counsel, especially in areas involving money. However, such counsel is available to anyone willing to take the time to follow sound principles to find a wise counselor.

PRINCIPLE 1: CHRISTIAN COUNSEL

Select your counselors on the basis of a common value system. For the Christian that means finding counselors who acknowledge Jesus Christ as their Savior and Lord. "How blessed is the man who does not walk in the counsel of the wicked, nor stand in the path of sinners, nor sit in the seat of scoffers" (Psalm 1:1). In no way does that imply non-Christians can't give good advice. Some of them give better advice than many Christians. But the standards by which decisions are made in our society are quite often incompatible with God's standards.

PRINCIPLE 2: WISE COUNSEL

"He who walks with wise men will be wise, but the companion of fools will suffer harm" (Proverbs 13:20). The mere fact that someone is a Christian, however, does not qualify him as an expert in every area of life. The evidence that Christians can and do give bad counsel is all too evident. The process of salvation does not eliminate attitudes of ego, pride, and greed in most of us.

Additionally many "Christian" counselors suffer from an acute lack of common sense. Wisdom comes from God, and in James 1:5 we are told, "But if any of you lacks wisdom, let him ask of God, who gives to all men generously." Both counselor and counselee must be in regular communication with God.

Most Christians have found that the majority of the decisions they face can be answered on the basis of God's written Word, and the wisdom they lack is the wisdom to understand (and accept) what God has already told them.

PRINCIPLE 3: MULTIPLE COUNSELORS

"Without consultation, plans are frustrated, but with many counselors they succeed" (Proverbs 15:22). No one can be expert enough in all areas of finance for anyone to depend upon his counsel exclusively. Any financial counselor who steers clients away from other qualified sources of advice is foolish. "He who walks with wise men will be wise, but the companion of fools will suffer harm" (Proverbs 13:20).

The areas of taxes, securities, stocks, bonds, and real estate are so complex that only with a variety of good counselors can you really get good advice. What inhibits most financial counselors from suggesting other advisers is the fear of losing a client or that a client will find out that he has received bad advice. Counselors who are good at what they do and seek the best for their clients have no reason to fear losing them.

HOW TO WEIGH COUNSEL

"The naive believes everything, but the prudent man considers his steps" (Proverbs 14:15). The purpose of counsel is to offer suggestions, alternatives, and options—not to make your decision for you. Even the best counsel in the world lacks an essential ingredient necessary to making decisions—God's plan for your life. Paul was given accurate, godly counsel not to return to Jerusalem in Acts 21. Paul listened and weighed that counsel against what God had impressed upon him to do and refused to be swayed from God's path.

Sometimes people call to ask what I think about some financial advice they have received. Often without offering any counsel at all, I ask them how they feel about the suggestion, and they respond, "I really don't have peace about doing it." If they had listened to their conscience, they would have already made the decision. The investment may be great, but it's not for them. Anything that robs us of God's peace is contrary to God's plan for us.

I have found many people who know a great deal more about their area of expertise than I do. Those people I use as resources. But I have found that even more people know practically nothing about the areas in which they give advice. Those people I try to avoid. The problem is that at first it's sometimes difficult to distinguish between the two groups.

TEST THEIR COUNSEL

When I'm evaluating someone's counsel in an area with which I am unfamiliar, I pick a subject about which we should both be knowledgeable and test him. If I find his answers to be fundamentally wrong in an area I do understand, I avoid his counsel in areas I don't understand.

COMPARE TO GOD'S WORD

In Proverbs 3:5 we are told to "trust in the Lord with all your heart." Any counsel that is contrary to God's Word should be counted worthless. Recently a friend was advised by his attorney to divorce his wife during a pending car accident lawsuit so that if she lost, she could file bankruptcy without endangering his assets. They could remarry later, he said, and everything would be all right. My advice was to divorce himself from that ungodly counsel.

TEST COUNSELOR'S VALUE SYSTEM

Proverbs 13:5 says that "a righteous man hates falsehood." A man who will deceive someone else on your behalf will eventually deceive you as well, given the right set of circumstances. Just because someone calls himself a Christian does not mean that he holds to God's value system.

TRACK RECORD

Proverbs 21:5 says, "The plans of the diligent lead surely to advantage." A good test of a counselor's expertise is his past performance. If every financial adviser were graded on the basis of promises versus performance, many would grade rather low. Any time you choose to invest time and money with someone who has less than five years of verifiable track record, you should assume that you're his on-the-job training.

ASK FOR REFERENCES

Few people ask for multiple references from a financial counselor, and even fewer verify those references. A friend once asked me to check out an investment salesman for him from his own list of references. The first reference spent ten minutes telling me what a poor job the man had done for him and ended up saying that he didn't even answer the salesman's calls anymore. Two more calls verified that this fellow never expected anyone to actually call a listed reference. Most people who list references try to list the best, so I assumed these were his best clients. Remember what Proverbs 21:29 says: "A wicked man shows a bold face." Most so-called "advisers" count on a good front to satisfy most clients.

How to Locate Good Counsel

The best method for locating good, Christian counsel is from other Christians who have been helped. Quite often if you ask others at your church someone will recommend a good resource. You can also call several pastors in your area. They almost always know of quality people in their communities. There are several Christian professional associations, such as the Christian Legal Society, the Christian Medical Association, and the Fellowship of Companies for Christ. Obviously not everyone involved with these associations is either Christian or expert, but they are good starting points. Without a doubt, the expert Christian counsel we need is available if we seek it diligently.

The Ten Keys to Better Investing

Even though every family's needs in the area of investing are different, there are certain common principles that can provide a solid foundation for anybody. I hesitate to label anything "1, 2, 3, 4, 5 . . . " because it may take the rest of your life to implement 1 and 2. Nevertheless, I have tried to distill the basic investing principles into ten keys, or guidelines. If you read and apply these to your own financial plans, your investment decisions will be easier.

KEY 1: FORMULATE
CLEAR-CUT INVESTMENT GOALS

No one should invest without an ultimate purpose for the money. You may be laying money aside for education or retirement, but you should have a clear-cut financial goal. I'd like to briefly discuss some realistic goals.

Retirement goal. There is nothing wrong with retirement planning, provided it is balanced. But in our society eighteen-year-olds look for a job with a good retirement plan. Many people look forward to retirement only because they hate their jobs.

You should always be where you can serve God best. If you are, retirement plans become less important. Obviously since you may not be able to do the same work at sixty-five or seventy that you're able to do at twenty-five or thirty, you may need to lay money aside now to supplement your income later. In fact, retirement savings can allow you to volunteer for a Christian organization without the need for a salary.

Your long-range retirement goal will vary depending on your age and income. If you're twenty-five, your perspective should be long-range growth and flexibility (diversity) of investments. What you need to invest per month is significantly less than that of someone aged forty-five.

This rule is true regardless of the long-range financial goal (retirement, education, and so on). The longer the time period in which to plan, the less initial money it takes. However, the criteria for long-range investing (such as hedging against inflation, depression, and financial collapse) are different than for immediate goals. Therefore the investments you would select for retirement forty years away are different than those you would select for retirement in ten years. A U.S. treasury bill paying 7 percent may perfectly fit the retirement plan for a sixty-five-year-old widow and yet be totally inappropriate for a thirty-year-old attorney.

According to the Social Security department, the average sixty-five-year-old man in America is worth about $100. In other words, if he cashed out all of his assets and liquidated all of his liabilities, he would be worth about $100.

Proverbs 6:6 says, "Go to the ant, O sluggard, observe her ways and be wise, which, having no chief, officer or ruler, prepares her food in the summer, and gathers her provision in the harvest." These are the harvest years of your life. Remember that the winter years are coming.

Preservation goal. Let's assume that you have inherited $100,000 and you want to preserve that money for a particular purpose at a later date, perhaps education, retirement, or a charitable donation. A couple starting out with $100,000 will have a different plan than a couple starting out from zero. A couple starting out at zero must first develop a surplus and then look for investments to help it grow. The couple with a $100,000 windfall should look first to preservation of the assets. Will Rogers once said, "I am not concerned so much with the return *on* my money as I am with the return *of* my money." Typically the investment program for a one-time windfall will be conservative. The goal is not to maximize the growth but to minimize losses and achieve a reasonable return.

Such is also the case for those who can put away sizable amounts from their incomes. Doctors are a good example. Most of the money that most doctors accumulate is earned through their primary profession, medicine. Most of what they lose is through speculative investments. The plan that is best for most doctors should be focused on the preservation of capital with a reasonable degree of growth to keep the value of their money current. They do not need high-risk investments.

Education goal. Unlike those who are trying to preserve a windfall, a family with the children's education in mind must think in terms of growth, again depending on the amount available to invest and the duration it can be invested.

Let's assume, for instance, that a couple can put aside $1,000 a year for the education of their children, who will reach college age in approximately ten years. The $10,000 they can save may not educate one child, much less two or three. So they're going to have to take some additional risks to achieve the growth they need.

This is the principle called "risk versus return." The higher the rate of return you need, the greater degree of risk you will have to assume. (This principle will be explained more fully below.)

Income goal. A couple entering retirement and looking for maximum income to live on will likely have this fourth objective. They need income, but they must also be concerned with the preservation of their assets. Once their needed income level is met, other assets can be invested to offset inflation. Let's assume that a couple is approaching retirement and they have $8,000 a year from Social Security, but they know that it will cost them $15,000 a year to live. Their primary concern is selecting investments that can earn $7,000 a year.

The risk they assume is determined by the $7,000 income they need. If they have $100,000 and need a 7-percent return, they will probably be able to use secure investments, such as U.S. treasury bills. But if they only have $50,000, T-bills won't do it. So they have to take some additional risks. Hopefully the more they know about investing, the lower the risk will be.

Growth goal. Everyone would like to have his or her investments grow. A growth strategy means that there is minimal immediate need for the funds but a sizable future need. Carried to the extreme, this strategy is called "get rich quick," in which case it is unscriptural. As Proverbs 28:22 says, "A man with an evil eye hastens after wealth, and does not know that want will come upon him."

A growth goal should be the strategy of someone fifty years of age who is able to save $1,000 a year toward retirement. The short period of time—fifteen years—and the limited funds —$1,000 a year—dictate an aggressive growth strategy.

This would also be the case of the couple with $10,000 to educate their children. They need an aggressive strategy that leans more toward risk-taking than preservation.

Tax shelter goal. The sixth and final goal in investing is tax sheltering. Tax sheltering is complex. In fact, over the last few years the federal government, through changes in the tax laws, has virtually shut down tax shelters, other than depreciation and interest for the average investor. It is often taught that paying interest is a good tax shelter, but that is an old wives' tale. When you pay interest to save income tax, you lose and the lender gains.

However, depreciation and investment tax credits can be legitimate tax shelters. An important principle to remember is that when you defer income tax through depreciation, you eventually must recapture it. Most tax shelters don't really eliminate income tax; they only defer it to a later time. For instance, if you put money into a retirement plan such as an IRA, it is an excellent tax shelter. You don't avoid the income taxes when you retire, but hopefully you pay them at a lower rate.

When you claim depreciation on rental property, you do not avoid paying income taxes. You defer them until a later period. When the property is sold, all of the depreciation that you claimed can be recaptured in income taxes. The only exception is if you use the property as a charitable gift; then you can claim a charitable deduction for the fair market value of the property and not have to repay the depreciated portion. Note: Frequent tax law changes can modify this deduction. The 1986 Tax Reform Act made such gifts subject to alternative minimum tax rules. Consult your CPA for details.

I could tell many horror stories about people I have counseled who thought they could outsmart the IRS. To my knowledge none succeeded. Most ended up paying the taxes plus interest and penalties and losing the investment money as well.

I recall a young real estate salesman named Carl who had been investing in apartment buildings with several other Christians from his church. Carl managed the complexes for which he received a monthly fee. The investors were allocated the tax write-offs for depreciation, taxes, interest, and so on.

As the buildings appreciated in value, Carl borrowed against the equity, sharing with his limited partners. He then raised the rents to cover the additional loan payments—a great strategy during good times.

But what Carl failed to realize was that he had created a time bomb just waiting for a slump in the economy. Inevitably that slump came, and renters who had lost their jobs moved out.

When the break-even point of 90 percent occupancy was passed, Carl quickly got into financial trouble. Within a few months the apartments were hopelessly delinquent and were being foreclosed by the lenders. After many struggles, with Carl desperately trying to find a way to salvage his investment, the apartments were repossessed. But that wasn't the end of Carl's troubles. The IRS declared that all of the previously claimed depreciation and equity loans would have to be recaptured, meaning that each of the investors would have to claim $50,000 in "phantom" income.

Many of the partners, including Carl, lost everything they owned and still owed thousands in taxes. Carl learned the hard way that you don't really avoid income taxes; you only delay them.

One final note about tax shelters. Never get into an investment solely for the tax benefits. Any good investment is eventually supposed to make money for you, and that is the true test that the IRS uses. Did you get into it primarily for economic benefit, or did you get into it primarily to save taxes? If it was to save taxes, the probability is that you're going to lose money in the investment, and you're going to pay back the income tax—with penalties. Remember the caution of Proverbs 28:20: "A faithful man will abound with blessings, but he who makes haste to be rich will not go unpunished."

KEY 2: AVOID PERSONAL LIABILITY

Most get-rich-quick schemes and tax shelters are available only if you accept personal liability for a large debt. God's Word says to avoid "surety," which means never make yourself personally liable for any indebtedness. For example, let's say you were going to buy a $10,000 piece of property but had only $2,000 as a down payment. So you put your $2,000 down on the property and then sign a note for the $8,000 that says, "If ever I can't pay the note, the lender has the right to recover his property and sue me for any deficiency." That is "surety"—taking on a personal liability without a certain way to pay.

On the other hand, let's assume that you're buying the same $10,000 piece of property. You put down your $2,000 and sign a note for the additional $8,000. But the note reads, "If ever I can't pay, the lender has the right to keep what I have already paid and recover his property, but I owe nothing additional." In other words, there is no personal liability for any deficiency. In legal terms that's "exculpatory," meaning that you have limited your liability to the collateral at risk. Thus, you have avoided surety because you always have a definite way to pay—surrender the property. That is the only biblically sound way to borrow.

I would counsel every Christian to avoid personal liability at all costs. Then if you buy equipment, property, or investments, the most you can lose is the money you have "at risk" and not future earnings. Failure to do this can result in the loss of all your family's assets. Many times when an investment goes bad, it does so during the worst times in the economy. That's usually when you are least capable of carrying the loss.

I recall an example from the mid 1970s in Atlanta. I was counseling two doctors who were partners together in various real estate ventures. They had the opportunity to buy an apartment complex for about half of its appraised value. All it required was a minimal down payment of $50,000 and signing for the mortgage, which was $1,000,000.

They assured me there was no way the investment could go bad because they could make money with the complex only 50 percent occupied, and it had never been less than 80 percent occupied. The only hitch was that they had to personally endorse the note. In other words, they personally indemnified the lender against any losses. Against my counsel, they both signed the note.

About two years later it was discovered that the complex had urea formaldehyde insulation in the walls and ceiling. It was condemned, and health officials required that the entire structure be torn down. The insurance paid for a portion of the loss but not everything. The doctors were able to sell the land for another portion. But when it was all finished, the two of them personally owed nearly half a million dollars.

One of the doctors went bankrupt. The other, who was a Christian, decided that he could not go bankrupt and committed to repay the loan. As best I know, he's still paying it. The investment itself was good. The deal was excellent. The only difficulty was that they had to sign personally, which is surety.

Remember the wisdom of Proverbs 22:26: "Do not be among those who give pledges, among those who become sureties for debts." Don't sign surety, no matter how good the deal sounds. (The booklet *Financial Freedom* in this series provides more suggestions for how to avoid debt.)

Sound Investments

Remember the "risk versus return" principle. The higher the rate of return, the higher the degree of risk. You can lower the risk through education and careful analysis, but you cannot eliminate it. The reason any investment pays a higher rate of return is because it must do so to attract the needed capital.

For instance, an insured CD or government note may pay 7 percent, whereas an equivalent corporate bond may pay 10 to 12 percent. Why does a corporate bond pay a higher interest rate? Because the risk in corporate bonds is higher than in government notes. Before investing in anything riskier than an insured savings account, you need to ask yourself this fundamental question: "Can I really afford to take this risk?"

The answer normally depends on two factors: your age and purpose. The older you are, the less risk you can afford to take because it's more difficult to replace the money. If the purpose of the money is retirement or education and both are still years away, you can probably afford to take a higher risk. However, if you need to live on the investment funds right now, you need the lower risk, regardless of your age.

If you are evaluating an investment with a relatively low return, your risk should be proportionately low as well. Treasury bills, treasury bonds, and certificates of deposit yield a relatively low rate of interest, but they also have a relatively low degree of risk, at least under normal economic circumstances.

If you find an investment that promises a high rate of return but advertises a low degree of risk, watch out. There are no free lunches. As Proverbs 14:18 says, "The naive inherit folly, but the prudent are crowned with knowledge."

KEY 4: KEEP SOME ASSETS DEBT-FREE

As a general rule, you should keep at least 50 percent of your investments debt-free. This also assumes you are following the guidelines of Key 2 and accept no surety. In other words, the money you have at risk in the investments is all you can lose.

The basic idea is to leverage about half of your investments—without personal liability—to hedge against inflation. Your money is actually multiplied through the leverage. With the other half of your investments debt-free, you can never lose everything.

Recently a friend in the real estate development business called to discuss a problem. His business had suffered a large slump due to the economy in his area. As a result of committing to a no-surety plan and keeping at least half of his assets debt-free, he could release the leveraged investments without losing everything.

But he called to ask for advice about selling some of the debt-free investments to help carry some of the other assets. I asked why he would consider selling the debt-free assets to pay on the others. He replied, "I have tens of thousands of dollars in those investments. I really hate to lose them." What he was about to do was exactly what his associates were doing, risking good assets to feed their debts. They had little choice because they had personally endorsed every loan and everything was at risk. But my friend had a choice.

He was literally gambling that the economy in his area would turn around before his assets were exhausted. My counsel was, "Don't risk good assets to feed loans. If they can't pay their way or be sold, let them go."

He followed that advice and is still in business whereas most of his associates have failed.

KEY 5: BE PATIENT

A smart investor keeps some cash on hand for emergencies so that he or she doesn't have to borrow, no matter what the economy does. As a general rule though, only about 5 to 10 percent of your investments should be in cash or near-cash investments. These include bonds, certificates of deposit, treasury bills, and money market funds.

It's important to get your money working for you, but patience will help avoid a great many errors. Most investments look good initially, even the bad ones. I have never heard of anyone advertising an investment as a really bad deal. Most salesmen sincerely believe in their products. It's up to you to sort out the good from the bad.

You must know what your goals and objectives are and only select the investments that help to meet them. Greed and speed often work together, so a key to avoiding greed is patience. As the proverb says, "A faithful man will abound with blessings, but he who makes haste to be rich will not go unpunished" (Proverbs 28:20).

Be cautious, and above all, be patient. "Rest in the Lord and wait patiently for Him" (Psalm 37:7). Before you do anything, talk about it, pray about it, and give God time to answer.

KEY 6: DIVERSIFY

An old adage says, "Don't put all your eggs in one basket," and that certainly applies to your investment strategy. Let's assume, for example, that you have a small amount of money to invest, say $1,000, and you want to buy some stock. If you put your $1,000 into one company's stock, all of your money rests on how that company does. An alternative is called a mutual fund. In a mutual fund your money is pooled with many others' and invested in a variety of companies. Therefore, you achieve diversification merely by selecting a mutual fund, as opposed to just buying stock in one company.

I would also suggest splitting your money into different areas of the economy. For example, one part might be in real estate, some in gold and silver, a percent in stocks and bonds, and the remainder in CDs. That helps to buffer you from cyclical ups and downs.

For instance, if the price of stock goes up and you have all of your money in the stock market, you'll do great. But if you hit a downturn in the stock market and you need to cash out, the result will be a significant loss. However, if you have only a portion of your money in the stock market, another portion in the bond market, some in real estate, some in gold and silver, and so on, the probability is that when one of these areas is down, another will be up. So rather than having to sell the one that's down, you could sell one that's up. Bernard Baruch had a wise saying: "When everybody else is buying, it's time to sell." You should strive to buck the trends rather than be forced to go with them.

Let me use another example. Assume you had $10,000 to invest. You might split the money, putting $5,000 into stocks and $5,000 into bonds. Assume the stocks are inflating because the economy is growing rapidly. Normally bonds are devalued as the economy expands, so you don't want to sell the bonds. If you needed cash, you'd sell some stock.

But if the economy reversed and interest rates went down rather than up, the stock could drop and the bonds improve in value. Obviously it's not always as ideal as my example implies because sometimes both stocks and bonds go sour at the same time. That's why further diversification is usually necessary.

It's important to remember that diversification is not a one-time decision. In other words, you don't diversify and then forget it. You have to continue managing your money. We are required to be stewards, managers of God's property. If you don't have the knowledge, you need to gain it. Spend an hour a day for six months studying any area of investing, and you'll know more than most people who sell it.

To diversify your investments you need to understand how a multi-tiered plan works. I'll demonstrate this system later in this booklet when we discuss specific investments, but briefly I use five tiers.

Tier 1 is secure income, such as CDs, stocks, government bonds, and notes.

Tier 2 is long-term income. These are investments that are higher risks but have a higher rate of return, such as mortgages, corporate bonds, and so on.

Tier 3 is growth investments, such as mutual funds, utility stocks, and gold funds.

Tier 4 is speculative growth investments, such as development property, limited partnerships, and new businesses.

Tier 5 is pure speculation investments, such as oil and gas, precious metals, and gemstones.

Depending on your age, income, and temperament, you may want to omit one or more of these levels in your planning. For instance, an older person may not want to get into tier 5, the purely speculative area. A younger person may not want to get into tier 1, the purely secure income. Some of the examples we'll look at should help clarify which levels fit best in different circumstances.

KEY 7: FOLLOW LONG-RANGE TRENDS

Invest with an eye to long-range economic trends, especially inflation. Many times we get trapped in following short-range trends. When the economy is doing well and inflation and interest rates are down, everything seems to be going great, so everybody wants to jump into the market and make a lot of money.

Some people who get in will make money, but the vast majority are going to panic during a short-term downturn and lose most or all of the money they made. In fact, if they chose to speculate, they may lose more than they made, especially if they borrowed to invest. When the market drops, they can't afford to ride it out, so they sell in a down market, as Black Monday in October 1987 demonstrated. It's always important to think in terms of long-term economics when you evaluate where to put your money. Remember that with long-term trends, whatever is happening right now will eventually reverse. Your investments should not stay stagnant, but don't panic. Bernard Baruch also said, "There is a strange phenomenon practiced by most investors, that most people tend to panic when their assets decline in value, and they will sell simply because they have not taken a long-range view of things."

Perhaps the most significant economic trend that has affected investments during the last ten years has been inflation, and over the next ten it will be either inflation or the threat of depression—or perhaps both. Our primary weapon in fighting a depression is the expansion of credit, which leads a full circle back to inflation again. So for the years 1990-2000, prudent investors who would like their resources to be available in the next decade must hedge against both possibilities of inflation and depression.

In noninflationary economy you can put your money in a treasury bill or certificate of deposit and stay even with the economy. But in an inflationary economy, unless you have your money at risk in things that are being inflated with the economy, your buying capacity is eroded.

For example, during the '70s the most inflation-vulnerable investments were stocks, bonds, savings accounts, treasury bills, and most other near-cash investments. Stocks proved vulnerable primarily because the inflation growth went to the real estate markets. The mid '80s saw the stock market recover some of the earlier inflationary growth but only at the price of great volatility.

The most inflation-proof investments throughout several decades have been real assets: things that you can use and touch such as land, metals, apartment buildings, or houses.

During the periods of inflation and low interest rates, many paper investments, such as stocks and bonds, do very well. During those times people tend to forget about inflation, which can be a costly mistake in a debt-run economy. When inflation turns around and interest rates increase to combat it, years of growth can be wiped out in a few months.

KEY 8: FOCUS ON WHAT YOU OWN

In 1975 I was counseling many people who had been wiped out during an economic downturn in the Atlanta area. Many were men who had a significant net worth. Unfortunately, most of their assets were tied up in liabilities and were illiquid. In other words, they didn't have any cash. Their assets were leveraged and required regular payments, and when the payments came due they couldn't pay and lost everything.

Almost exactly the same happened in the oil industry in the mid 1980s. Men whose net worth was in the millions lost everything they owned, including their homes.

I recall an oilman I met in the late '70s. He was a committed believer and a member of the Christian Oilmen's Association. He had got into the oil business just before the oil embargo and had seen the price of oil go from about $6 a barrel to more than $30. It seemed that everything he touched turned to gold, and he was thoroughly hooked on the Christian "prosperity message." He literally believed that his giving guaranteed him immunity from economic problems.

As I got to know him I found that he was worth millions through the oil leases as well as several drilling operations. But everything was leveraged to the limit. He used every increase in oil prices to borrow more against his reserves so that he could expand further.

When I challenged him on the principle of surety, he became defensive and ducked behind the normal Christian escape, "God told me to do it." He said he prayed regularly about every decision, and God confirmed his actions through the increases in his assets. He had also adopted a good-economy mentality. He believed the economy would continue to inflate and carry oil prices with it. What he didn't realize was that much of the inflation was due to the increasing oil prices.

The early '80s saw the price of oil plummet as the oil cartel fell apart. At the same time President Ronald Reagan waged a war against inflation through high interest rates to choke off the money supply. About this time worldwide conservation began to reduce the demand for oil. This triple blow crippled the oil industry.

The mainline companies such as Shell, Texaco, and Gulf did fine with their pre-inflation oil leases, but most of the new ventures were wiped out, including that Christian oilman. He could have cashed out in 1979 with perhaps $20 million; yet in 1986 he saw his home and furnishings auctioned off by the court.

You see, net worth doesn't mean anything. It's how much you actually own unencumbered by liabilities. Again, it is important to have a goal that at least half of your assets will be totally debt-free. How can you do that? By deciding, "The next time I sell an investment, I'll use that to pay off another investment." As the Lord said, "For which one of you, when he wants to build a tower, does not first sit down and calculate the cost, to see if he has enough to complete it?" (Luke 14:28).

KEY 9:   KNOW WHERE TO SELL

Before you buy, always know where you can sell the investment. This key is important when you're dealing with so-called "exotic investments," such as gemstones, silver, gold, or collectibles. You can do well buying these items if you know what you're doing. But most people who buy collectibles have no idea of where or how to sell them.

Let's assume that you bought gold in bullion form. Unless you have an agreement with the sales company that they will buy it back from you, you may have a difficult time even selling your gold. If you do sell it and gold is being quoted for, say, $400 an ounce, you will discover that a broker won't give you that much for it. In fact, he may offer as little as $350 an ounce, even though it's certified bullion. Why? Because he needs to make a commission on it too.

Other collectibles, such as figurines, paintings, stamps, and coins, are difficult for a novice to sell profitably. When you invest in these items, you need to have a clear understanding of how and where you can resell them. I have counseled many people who said, "Well, the salesman told me that if I ever wanted to resell, he would buy it back." Then later they find out that their salesman is no longer around. Be sure you know an alternate sales source in the event that the salesman or company you buy through is gone. Even if they have been in business for fifty years, they can still fold. Usually investors are better off staying with less exotic investments that have multiple markets available.

KEY 10: TRAIN FAMILY MEMBERS

Every family member should be trained in the principles of sound investing.

Statistically in America a wife outlives her husband about 85 percent of the time. That's an important key to remember when developing an investment portfolio. Most widows, especially young widows, have no concept of how to manage any kind of investment program. Many times because they don't understand the investments, they liquidate at the wrong time and suffer significant losses. A wife needs to be trained in good money management and investment strategy. She needs to know how to buy and sell and where to go for the help she needs. It is poor stewardship for a wife not to understand the investment portfolio.

Also, since it is not uncommon for a husband and wife to die together in an accident, the older children should be brought into family decisions involving your investments. At a minimum, you need to leave them instructions so that they will be able to manage your portfolio without having to dispose of it upon your death just to pay estate taxes.

DEVELOPING AN INVESTMENT STRATEGY

Before you invest your hard-earned money, take the time to analyze the different types of investments available, and decide which best suit your short- and long-term financial plans. "The plans of the diligent lead surely to advantage, but everyone who is hasty comes surely to poverty" (Proverbs 21:5).

In order to gain a thorough understanding of the principles involved in investing, a few definitions are in order. First, both income and growth are included under the general term *return*. In other words, you may have cash income from a certificate of deposit or growth income from a rental house. Both are considered return on investment. The first is immediate, and the second is long-term. Income is the average current yearly yield. Growth refers to the average yearly appreciation of the underlying investment. So if you get a 5-percent cash return from a rental house after all expenses are paid and the house is also appreciating at 5 percent per year, it has a 10-percent per year return on investment.

The term *risk* refers to potential loss. In other words, all things being equal, what is the probability that you will get your money back on an investment? To measure risk and return—income and growth are rated separately—I have simply assigned a scale from 0 to 10 that can be applied to each type of investment. Zero represents the least return or the least risk, and 10 represents the highest risk or highest return. Therefore, an investment with an income potential of 0 and a risk factor of 10 would represent the worst possible investment. An investment with an income potential of 10 and a risk of 0 would be the best investment. (You can't find those, by the way.)

Investments are divided into five basic types.

1. Secure Income: selected because it generates cash
2. Long-Term: selected for duration of earnings
3. Growth Investments: selected primarily for long-term appreciation
4. Speculative Growth: a mix between growth and speculation
5. Pure Speculation: high-risk investments selected for their volatility and growth potential

Please remember that the rating for each type of investment is purely my opinion. Time and economic conditions constantly change, and the degree of return or risk for most types of investments change with the economy. When interest rates and inflation are high, real property, residential housing, apartment complexes, or office buildings generally do well. But when interest rates and inflation are down, stocks and bonds generally do well.

TYPE 1: SECURE INCOME INVESTMENTS

These investments primarily generate income.

Government securities: income 5, growth 0, risk 1. Treasury bills (T-bills), Government National Mortgage

Association bonds (Ginnie Mae), and savings bonds fall into this category.

Bank securities: income 5, growth 0, risk 3-4. One advantage of bank investments such as savings accounts, certificates of deposit (CDs), and insured money funds is that you can get them with smaller amounts of money. It generally takes $10,000 to $25,000 to purchase a treasury bill, but you can purchase a CD for as little as $500. The disadvantages are that they offer no growth; the payout is fixed and income is all taxable.

Be certain that you invest with a bank protected by the FDIC, a savings and loan protected by the FSLIC, or a credit union insured up to $100,000. If worst comes to worst, the government will print the money to pay what it owes. If you are going to risk your money long-term and have a choice between a government security or a bank note, I recommend the government security because it has the same income and less risk.

TYPE 2:
LONG-TERM INCOME INVESTMENTS

There are six major types of long-term investments.

Municipal bonds: income 5, risk 7-8. These are bonds issued by a particular municipality, such as Denver, Atlanta, or Chicago. The primary selling point is that most or all of the income from municipal bonds is exempt from federal income tax and isn't normally subject to state income tax in the state where they are issued.

The liabilities of municipal bonds are: (1) they have low yields; (2) they normally require a large initial investment; and (3) they are illiquid, meaning that if you have to sell them, you will normally do so at a loss. With the exception of buying some municipal bonds for diversification, most people are better off with government bonds.

Mortgages: income 8, growth 0, risk 3-4. A mortgage is a contract under which you lend someone the money to buy a home or other real property, and you hold the first mortgage rights to it. One way to arrange this is to find someone who has financed a first mortgage and wants to sell it to get his money out. The seller normally discounts the mortgage to yield from 3 to 5 percent above the prevailing interest rates. So if current interest rates on CDs are 7 percent, you could earn 10 to 12 percent through a first mortgage.

The risk on this type of investment is low because you have real property backing up your money. If a borrower fails to pay, you can foreclose on the property. The key here is the value of the property securing the mortgage. I suggest that any investment in a first mortgage be backed with property valued at two to three times the outstanding loan.

The liabilities of this kind of investment are: (1) they are hard to find—it's usually necessary to know a local attorney or banker who handles them; (2) the return on your investment is 100 percent taxable; (3) there is no growth on your principal, unless interest rates drop, in which case your mortgage might be worth more; and (4) your money will be tied up for a long time, usually fifteen to twenty years.

If you're looking for long-term income, a first mortgage is a good way to invest. If you're selling property that you own debt-free, consider taking a first mortgage for the amount you were going to invest for income purposes. You can earn a higher rate of interest with less risk than virtually any other investment.

Corporate bonds: income 6-8, growth 0, risk 5-6. A corporate bond is a note issued by a corporation to finance its operation. Some bonds pay a rate of 2 to 3 percent higher than a CD or T-bill. The amount of return depends on the rating of the company issuing the bond. Bonds are rated from a low of "C" to a high of "AAA." The higher the grade of the bond, the lower the rate of return, but the risk is lower as well.

Many investors prefer bonds that generate current income through business operations, such as utility company bonds. In the past, utility company bonds have been stable and predictable. However, many utilities have suffered massive debts from nuclear power station construction, making them greater risks. In general, most utility bonds are safe investments.

Corporate bonds depend on the success of one company. If that company defaults, the assets of the entire company can be attached—including your bond. Another liability is that the income is 100 percent taxable. A bond has little chance for growth unless your rate of return is in excess of the current interest rates.

Insurance annuity: income 3-4, risk 5-6. This investment requires you to pay a prescribed amount of money into the annuity. Then the insurance company promises you an income each month after you retire.

Annuities (1) provide tax-deferred income—the earnings are allowed to accumulate tax-deferred until you retire; (2) the investment is fairly liquid, so if you have to get your money out you can, although there is often a penalty; and (3) compared to other tax-sheltered investments, the returns are good.

But be aware that sometimes the percentage given is a gross figure from which sales and administrative costs are deducted. It's best to ask for a net figure to do your comparisons and get all quotes in writing from the agent offering the annuity.

Stock dividends: income 4-5, risk 6-7. Common stocks usually pay dividends based on the earnings of the company. You can buy stocks for relatively small amounts of money. It's possible to invest in a stock paying a dividend of 7 to 8 percent and only risk $25. This appeals to the small investor. Since the dividend is totally related to the success of the issuing company, I would look for a company that has paid dividends for many years, particularly during hard times.

I personally believe the liabilities of relying on stock dividends for income outweigh the advantages. For one thing, all stock dividends ultimately depend on the company's profits. Even if a corporation has paid dividends for decades, that doesn't necessarily mean it will continue to do so. The automobile industry in the early 1980s is a good example. Some of the companies that paid high rates of return for three and four decades had to cut their returns drastically. The people who depended on the dividends went through some lean times. So, if you plan to invest in stocks for income, you need to assess the degree of risk.

Money funds: income 4-5, risk 2-8. Money funds are the pooled savings accounts of many people used to purchase short-term securities. These are not true savings accounts but short-term mutual funds that pay interest. Most are not insured against losses. Money funds are available through most brokerage firms, savings and loans, and banks. The interest rates vary according to current interest rates.

TYPE 3: GROWTH INVESTMENTS

This tier is in the middle and represents the crossover from conservative to speculative investments. During one cycle of the economy these investments appear to be conservative, but during the next cycle they may be speculative.

Farmland: income 0-2, growth 6-7, risk 3-4. During the highly inflationary 1970s, farmland was a hot investment. People speculated in farmland just as they did in commercial real estate. This drove prices up. The 1980s saw inflation subside and farm prices level out. Consequently, farmland prices also fell. Today an investment in farmland is considered conservative, although there is a fair amount of risk, and any real growth is viewed as ten or more years away. This can and will change again as the economy changes.

Housing: income 5-7, risk 3-4. No investment during the last twenty-five years has been consistently better for the average investor than single-family rental housing. That doesn't mean it will stay that way forever, but I can see no long-range trends away from rental housing.

Housing costs are out of the price range of the average young couple, and since they have to live somewhere, most of them are going to rent, at least temporarily. One advantage of investing in rental housing is that you can do it with a relatively small initial down payment. If you take on the liability of a rental house, be sure not to accept surety for it. If the house won't stand for its own mortgage, pass it by.

Most rental housing not only generates income but also offers tax shelter through depreciation, interest, and taxes. The 1986 Tax Reform Act placed limits on what can be deducted for tax purposes against ordinary income, and it is entirely possible that future tax changes will affect real property even more. I still believe that rental housing promises good growth through the end of this century, barring economic catastrophe.

On the other hand, there are several negatives to rental housing: (1) If you don't want to be a landlord, don't buy rental housing. (2) If you aren't able to maintain and manage the property, many of the tax benefits decline. (3) It's not always easy to get your money out if you need it.

You may want to consider getting into a duplex or triplex. If you don't have the money to do this by yourself, you can invest in limited partnerships offered by individuals who purchase and manage duplexes and triplexes, or you can invest with another person. The advantage of owning a duplex or triplex is that your income isn't limited to one renter. In a single-family home if your renter moves, you have 100 percent vacancy.

The liabilities with duplexes or triplexes are that they require a bigger investment, more maintenance, and you really do become a landlord.

Remember the three key factors about buying any rental property, whether it be a single-family house, duplex, or triplex: location, location, and location.

TYPE 4:
SPECULATIVE GROWTH INVESTMENTS

There are three major types of speculative growth investments.

Mutual funds: income 5-7, risk 4-5. A mutual fund is an investment into which many small investors pool their money, and a group of professional advisers invest it for them, usually in the stock or bond markets. Specialized mutual funds invest in automobiles, precious metals, utility companies, government securities, and so on.

Mutual funds are valuable to the small investor for several reasons: (1) You can risk a relatively small amount of money—many mutual funds require as little as $25 to invest. (2) Your money is spread over a large area in the economy. (3) The return on good mutual funds has averaged more than twice the prevailing interest rates for any ten-year period.

I would encourage any potential investor in mutual funds to go to independent sources and check out the fund first. Two sources I use regularly and highly recommend are *Money* magazine and *Consumer Reports*. Both publish an annual review of mutual funds.

Christians need to be aware that some mutual funds invest in areas that are questionable and in some that are blatantly anti-Christian, including pornography, liquor, and abortion clinics. You should get a prospectus from the mutual fund that you're considering and find out where your money is going.

Another type of mutual fund invests in the bond market. These are primarily designed for income. I prefer mutual bond funds to buying individual corporate bonds because you spread out the risk. Mutual funds invest in many corporations, and the failure of one corporation is not going to significantly affect their—or your—income.

There are different fee structures for mutual funds, and the fees can be quite substantial. If you don't plan to leave your money in a mutual fund for at least five years, you probably shouldn't get into one.

Some are called "loaded funds"; others are "no-load funds." A loaded fund requires the service cost or commission to be paid up front. A no-load fund means they recover the fees over a number of years. The fees for load and no-load funds will be about the same over any five-year period.

I prefer the no-load fund because it allows my money to earn dividends without the service fees or commissions coming out of the initial investment. But either type will penalize you if you decide to withdraw your money during the first five years.

Common stocks: income 2-8, risk 7-8. Again, the advantage of common stocks is that you can invest with a relatively small amount of money, and there is potential for sizable growth. The liabilities of common stocks are obvious. First, you can suffer a loss as easily as you can make a profit. Second, stocks require buying and selling to maximize their potential. Most people think they can put their money into a stock and just let it sit without having to manage it, but that is rarely the case today. If you expect to make money in the stock market, you have to manage it. If you're not willing to do that, it's best to stay with other investments.

Precious metals: income 5-6, risk 8-9. Precious metals such as gold, silver, or platinum can be purchased either for long-term growth or pure speculation. For long-term growth, buy the metal, put it in a safety deposit box, and hope it appreciates over a period of time. Most people do this primarily as a hedge against a potential calamity in the economy. In an economy as unstable as ours, a small percentage of your assets invested in precious metals can be a good balance to assets more vulnerable to inflation. When buying and selling anything, especially precious metals, it's wise to remember what Baruch said: "Buy when they sell. Sell when they buy." Keep a long-term mentality about precious metals, at least those you invest in as a hedge.

Both gold and silver fluctuate with the economy. Gold usually cycles faster and further than silver. In general, the cycles of gold run the opposite of the U.S. dollar, so watch the dollar's trends for clues to the price of gold.

Limited partnerships: income 6-7, risk 8-9. You can form a limited partnership by pooling your money with another group of investors to purchase an investment, usually in real properties. The investment is managed by a general partner who has the authority to make buying and selling decisions. Since your investment in a limited partnership is no better than the property and the management, the key is to know the general partner and his credibility. Be confident in his ability to acquire and manage the properties.

As a limited partner, your liability is normally limited only to the amount of money that you have at risk. If a limited partnership requires subsequent annual payments, avoid it because it carries a contingent liability. You should limit your liability to the money that you have at risk. In the past, limited partnerships in properties such as apartment complexes, office complexes, or shopping centers were excellent investments because they sheltered other income. However, since 1987 most of those benefits have been gradually eliminated, and the tax write-offs can be used only to shelter passive income. For most investors, the risk is high.

TYPE 5: PURE SPECULATION

These investments should play a relatively small part—5 to 10 percent at the most—in any investment plan. Their primary value is their sizable potential appreciation; in other words, speculation. Most generate little or no income and are highly volatile.

Gold/Silver: income—incalculable, risk 9-10. Not only can you invest in precious metals for long-term growth, but you can also invest in gold and silver for short-term speculation. This would be most beneficial in a highly volatile economy where major changes are occurring, such as the oil crisis in the mid 1970s.

Obviously, such events are difficult to predict and are extremely risky. They are for the investor with a strong heart and cash only. Unless you are a professional investor, this is probably not an area where you want to risk a lot of money.

Oil and gas: income 7-8, risk 9-10. In the late '70s and early '80s when crude oil prices cycled up, oil and gas investments were the hottest things going. But many people investing money in oil and gas didn't understand the risks involved, and the vast majority lost their investments when the prices fell and marginal wells became unprofitable. There is a high degree of risk, particularly in oil exploration.

Many people invested in oil and gas limited partnerships to develop known gas and oil fields. Not only did they lose their money on these investments, but they also discovered they were liable for environmental damages caused by the wells. This kind of investment is not only risky but usually expensive as well. I believe the income potential for oil and gas over the next ten to fifteen years is excellent, but if you plan to invest in oil and gas only risk a small portion of your assets, and don't let anybody talk you into risking larger amounts.

Commodities market: income 10 plus, risk 10 plus. Commodities speculation requires a relatively small dollar investment and can bring high profits, primarily through the use of leverage. A $1,000 investment in the commodities market can control $10,000 worth of contracts—or more—for future delivery. If that sounds good, remember this: "A fool and his money are soon parted." Approximately one out of every two hundred people who invest in the commodities market ever gets any of his money back. That doesn't mean he made a profit—that means *any* of his money back. Investing in commodities is probably the closest thing to gambling that most people ever try. In fact, it is gambling. You can lose everything you own and more.

Collectibles: income 10 plus, risk 10 plus. Antiques, old automobiles, paintings, figurines, and so on are all collectibles that can be used while you hold them to sell. One of the most important prerequisites to investing in collectibles is knowledge. You need to know value before investing. Second, you need to put some time and labor into locating the best places to buy and sell. Third, you must have the capital to wait for just the right buyer. Often novice investors get discouraged and sell out at a loss.

Unless you have a high degree of knowledge in this area, the risk is inordinately high. With most items you can develop the expertise you need by talking with other people and reading. The rate of return on collectibles can easily be 10 plus, but the risk of loss is just as great.

Undeveloped land: income 8-9, risk 10 plus. In the late '70s and early '80s, buying undeveloped land to hold for development in growth areas was a great way to make money. The advantage of this kind of investment is that it has utility. For instance, if you buy residential lots to sell to potential home owners, even if the market for undeveloped lots is not doing well, it's possible to team up with a residential builder who will build on your lots and pay you as the homes sell.

Precious gems: You can buy diamonds, opals, rubies, sapphires, and other stones for relatively small amounts of money. You can have them mounted into a ring or pendant and wear them while you're waiting for them to appreciate. The potential risks are high. For every person I know who has made money in gems, I know a hundred who have lost money. It's difficult to tell quality gems from average ones. It's almost impossible for a novice to know the true value of a gem, even with a "certified" appraisal. Second, it's difficult to sell gems at a fair price unless you have your own market. The rule here is to stay with what you know or with someone you thoroughly trust.

This basic review of the five major types of investments is by no means exhaustive, but I trust it has provided pointers to get started in an investment strategy once you have your budget under control and develop a surplus.

Many good materials are available such as books on investing that you can check out of most public libraries. Remember that balance is the key, and be careful about whose advice you take, because so many people are dedicated to the leverage principle. Evaluate the risk involved with every investment. The higher the promised return, the higher the degree of risk, and the only way you can lower the risk is through your own personal expertise. You have to know what you're doing.

AVOIDING GET-RICH-QUICK SCHEMES

Every year thousands of Christian families risk and lose money they cannot afford to lose by seeking that "big deal." Can that loss be avoided? Most certainly, but not on the basis of human wisdom. There has never been a get-rich-quick scheme that didn't sound terrific on the surface. The promoters are a great deal better at disguising the bad deals than most people are at detecting them. Most get-rich-quick schemes rely on greed and quick decisions. There are three basic elements of any get-rich-quick scheme.

1. *Attract people who don't know what they're doing.* When you invest in areas you know nothing about, it's difficult to evaluate an investment. Christians are often gullible and prone to follow the recommendations of other Christians who don't know what they're doing either.

2. *Encourage people to risk money they cannot afford to lose.* Most people are more cautious with money they have earned than with money they borrow. Borrowed money comes so easily that it's "easy" to risk.

3. *Attract people who will make investment decisions on the spot.* That's why so many get-rich-quick plans rely on group meetings and a lot of emotional hype. I have found that if you hear of a deal that sounds so good that you don't want to wait and pray about it, pass it up. Good investments are rare and seldom flashy.

I remember a young computer salesman named Chad who called me about a deal "too good to pass up." He called me only because his wife pressured him into it. "But we have to see you right away," he said, "I've got to move quickly." So I scheduled a time to see them the next day.

Chad had a friend who knew a hotshot computer specialist in Colorado who had developed a program to do stock market trades between the U.S. and European stock exchanges and make profits on the differences.

He was taking in investors and making more than 10 percent per month for them. Chad had already cashed in his retirement plan and was about to borrow against the equity in their home. He calculated that he could make enough to start his own business within a couple of years.

His wife panicked to think that he was about to risk $25,000 with someone he didn't even know. Chad said he had talked with several other investors who were making lots of money. He said the developer had paid exactly what he promised every month.

My question was, "Why does he need your money if he's able to make more than 100 percent per year? Why doesn't he just borrow the money at 10 percent?"

Chad answered, "He wants Christian investors so that he can get into other ventures in the future." By experience I have found that any investment targeted primarily at Christians is worthy of some suspicion. So I asked Chad if he would mind if I checked this person out.

"No," he replied but then asked how long it would take because he had to make a decision quickly or the opportunity would be closed. I shared the biblical principles of get-rich-quick schemes with Chad, but it fell on deaf ears. His decision was made. I was just a necessary step to pacify his wife.

In my investigations I could find nothing on this computer trading genius. If he had learned his trade by handling stocks and bonds, nobody knew about it. I called to get a financial statement, and it was "on the way." But I never got even the slightest documentation on what he was doing.

In the meantime Chad invested $25,000 in this venture and received a check for $3,000 for the first month's profits. The next month he was offered the option of reinvesting the profits, which he did over my objections. He never received the third month's distribution because the state securities commissioner impounded all the "trader's" assets, pending an investigation for securities fraud. It seems that he had not been trading stocks at all. He had simply been raising money from gullible people—a lot of them.

The system was pretty simple. He paid dividends by raising more money each month. Once someone had received a month or so of distributions he was "allowed" to reinvest his profits, which most did. As long as the circle of investors kept expanding, he had no problems making the payments and pocketing a huge profit. His only overhead was a computer to keep up with the payments.

What blew the whistle was an investor who tried to talk his brother-in-law into investing too. But his brother-in-law was a security investigator who knew a scam when he saw one. Before he folded, this shyster had raised more than $20 million and had a list of clients that read like a Who's Who in entertainment, sports, and business.

STICK WITH WHAT YOU KNOW

"By wisdom a house is built, and by understanding it is established" (Proverbs 24:3). A great part of wisdom is recognizing our limitations.

Seldom is anyone duped into a get-rich-quick scheme in his area of expertise. It would be difficult to convince a chicken farmer that someone could get rich quickly in the chicken business.

DON'T RISK BORROWED MONEY

"A prudent man sees evil and hides himself, the naive proceed and pay the penalty" (Proverbs 27:12). It's one thing to speculate with money you can afford to lose and quite another to lose money that literally belongs to someone else. The former is called speculation; the latter is surety. That doesn't necessarily mean the investment should be paid in total, but it does mean that the down payment should not be borrowed.

The only time an investment should be financed (leveraged) is when there is adequate value to cover any liability or when payments can be made from a known source of funds and are not dependent on the sale of the investment. Otherwise, you are presuming on an uncertain event.

BUY INVESTMENTS WITH UTILITY

"She considers a field and buys it; from her earnings she plants a vineyard. . . . She makes linen garments and sells them, and supplies belts to the tradesmen" (Proverbs 31:16, 24). Utility simply means buying something of use to someone else. Most get-rich-quick schemes deal with intangibles or at least remote tangibles, such as oil wells, chicken farms, movies, motivational programs, and so on.

DON'T MAKE QUICK DECISIONS

"The plans of the diligent lead surely to advantage, but everyone who is hasty comes surely to poverty" (Proverbs 21:5). The very essence of a get-rich-quick scheme is emotionalism. Above all else, a get-rich-quick scheme depends on convincing the prospect to buy without thinking about it too long.

Get-rich-quick schemes always look great initially. If they didn't, nobody would buy them. To avoid these financial traps, you must establish your standards by God's Word: seek God's plan for your life, stick with what you know, seek good counsel, and wait on God's peace before acting.

"It is the blessing of the Lord that makes rich, and He adds no sorrow to it" (Proverbs 10:22).

Other Materials by Larry Burkett:

Books in this series:

Financial Freedom
Sound Investments
Major Purchases
Insurance Plans
Giving and Tithing
Personal Finances

Other Books:

Debt-Free Living
Financial Planning Workbook
How to Manage Your Money
Your Finances in Changing Times

Videos:

Your Finances in Changing Times
Two Masters
How to Manage Your Money
The Financial Planning Workbook

Other Resources:

Financial Planning Organizer
Debt-Free Living Cassette